So You are a Believer...

Who has been through Divorce...

A Myth-Busting Biblical Perspective on Divorce

Joseph J. Pote

So You are a Believer...Who has been through Divorce...
A Myth-Busting Biblical Perspective on Divorce

DEDICATION

This book is dedicated to the Overcomers Sunday School Class of Calvary Baptist Church in Hope, Arkansas.

Each of you is truly an inspiration to me!

Your prayers, encouragement and support mean more than you know.

Thank you for listening to my meandering lessons and for encouraging me to compile my notes into a book.

CONTENTS

ACKNOWLEDGMENTS

To my wife, Sherri, for being so supportive of my writing this book, for reviewing and offering such practical advice, and for being so patient with my obsessive writing and rewriting on weekends and evenings.

To my sister, Dorcas, for such enthusiastic encouragement and support.

To my sister, Deborah, for very thorough reviews and honest feedback. The message of this book is written more clearly as a result of our open discussion of topics on which we both have strong opinions.

To my mother-in-law, Belinda Mercer, for her review and feedback, as well as encouragement.

To Terry Kirkpatrick, both for encouragement and for assistance with editing.

To my pastor, Hal Dixon, for supporting my efforts with thorough reading of manuscripts and sound advice on strengthening discussion points and improving the flow of reading.

To Kay Arthur, Co-CEO, Author and Speaker for Precept Ministries International, PO Box 182218, Chattanooga TN 37422. Though I have never met Kay, personally, her *Precepts* Bible studies and her book, *Our Covenant God*, have greatly influenced my understanding of biblical covenants.

Introduction

What does Jesus look like going through a divorce?

This is the question I was faced with, in the summer of 2001, as a marriage to which I had devoted much effort and many prayers finally drew to an end.

As a Christian, I have set a life goal of learning to be conformed to the image of Christ, of trying to remember to face each life circumstance as Jesus would face it. Although I frequently fall short of the goal, my constant prayer is for God to change my heart, helping me to see each situation through His eyes, and to act accordingly.

As a father, I want to be the sort of father to my children that God is to us. As a husband, I want to love my wife as Christ loves the church. As an employee I want to serve my employer as Christ has served us. As a friend, I want to be the sort of friend that Jesus is to me.

Do I fall short of the goal? Of course I do! But, I come a lot closer than if I didn't set the goal and prayerfully pursue it. Our Heavenly Father seems to derive great joy in giving His children a new perspective, and is quick to respond to sincere prayers asking for a godly view of a given situation.

So, in finding myself facing divorce, I went before the Father, in earnest prayer. "Lord," I prayed, "show me what Jesus looks like going through a divorce. Please, help me to live my life, through this divorce, as You would."

No sooner were the words out of my mouth, than a rebuke sprang to mind, "Jesus would not *be* in a divorce!"

Oh, I cannot express how much that self-rebuke stung, or how disoriented it left me feeling! I had made it my life goal to try, in all circumstances, to learn to be like Christ. Now, I found myself in a life circumstance which I had never expected to be in, a circumstance in which I simply could not (at that time) picture Jesus ever being. How could I gain a godly perspective to act as Jesus would, if I was in a situation which Jesus would never be in? How could I invite God into a situation that I saw as ungodly?

Not knowing what else to do, I simply continued to pray, "God, please show me the way! Please help me to live my life the way You would want me to live it. Please, God, somehow, in the midst of this darkness, shine the light of Your glory, through my life."

In the weeks and months that followed, as I continued to make this my daily prayer, the Holy Spirit began recalling to my mind familiar Bible stories and scriptures, in a fresh new light.

A few years earlier, I had participated in several of the *Precepts* Bible studies developed by Kay Arthur, and had read Kay's book, *Our Covenant God*. Through Kay Arthur's classes and books, I had gained a clearer understanding of biblical covenants and had begun watching for covenant terminology and covenant references in my daily Bible reading.

Now, as the Holy Spirit ministered to me, I began to recall many familiar scriptures in a new light of covenant understanding. Familiar passages began to take on fresh new meaning to me, as I began to recognize their significance from a perspective of covenant and redemption. Out of this new perspective, a new understanding of God's view of marriage and divorce began to emerge. I began to realize that much of what I had believed about God's view of divorce was simply incorrect. I had accepted certain myths as truth, based not on scripture, but on words, actions, attitudes and impressions observed as a child, growing up in church.

In the years following that divorce, in conversing with other Christians with similar divorce experiences, I discovered that I was not alone in those misperceptions. In fact, these same myths are widely believed and accepted as truth by many people within the Christian church. For believers who have experienced divorce, these myths directly interfere with our relationships, acting as barriers as we seek to draw close to God, as well as to our fellow believers.

In the following chapters, we will explore some of these myths regarding divorce, comparing each of them to the truth of God's word, looking at each verse in context of the entire passage, as well as in context of the Bible as a whole.

This book is intended to expose error as error, while highlighting scriptural truth and biblical concepts regarding divorce. I pray that God will use this book to liberate fellow believers who have experienced divorce to a greater fullness of joy in the love and redemption of our God and Savior, Jesus Christ.

Prelude ~
Covenant and Redemption

Covenant and *redemption* are biblical concepts that were once very familiar in many ancient civilizations, but are much less familiar in modern western civilization. In our modern western society, the primary relationship that we still recognize in covenant terms is the covenant of marriage. Modern weddings retain many of the ancient traditions of covenant ceremony, and the vows are generally made with solemn awareness of the sacredness of the marriage covenant.

In fact, many of the ancient covenant traditions have been retained in modern wedding ceremonies despite their meaning having been largely forgotten. Consider the tradition of the bride and groom cutting the wedding cake and feeding it to each other. How many couples are aware that they are acting out an ancient rite of covenant, breaking bread and feeding it to each other, in a symbolic act of partaking of each other's nature, "this is my body" (Matthew 26:26)?

While the Bible specifically addresses the relatively narrow topic of divorce of a marriage covenant, it has much more to say on the broader topic of covenants in general. Not only does scripture provide superb examples of how God intends a covenant to be honored, but it also provides rich illustrations on the concept of redemption from a covenant that has become abusive bondage – a concept that is fundamental to the Christian faith. As we explore God's heart toward His children who have experienced divorce, we will draw on the full scriptural background of God's view of covenant and redemption.

Our God, the God of the Bible, is a covenant God. God invites those He loves to enter into covenant with Him, then faithfully acts on the basis of His covenant promises. God remembers His covenant promises to His children, and eternally lavishes His loving-kindness on those with whom He is in a covenant relationship. Through covenant relationship, God imparts His nature to us, and causes our hearts to be conformed to His image. All of God's interaction with mankind is based on covenant.

God created man in His own image. We, as His creation, as His children, as His covenant partners, are to honor and live out our covenants in faithfulness, just as He honors and lives out His covenants.

However, God never uses covenant as a tool to enslave or abuse, nor does He desire for His children to be enslaved in a covenant that has become abusive bondage. For His children who have become enslaved in abusive relationships, God offers redemption from covenants of bondage.

The most common definition provided for the word *redemption* is *to buy back*. However, in studying the use of this word in scripture, this simplified definition is found lacking.

While it does provide a nice simple definition for many instances of scriptural redemption, it does not adequately define the word as used in the most significant biblical redemptions. A more accurate definition of *redemption*, as used in scripture, would be *to justly bring about the end of a covenant of bondage by which someone or something belonging to God is being held captive.*

The Bible presents a fascinating narrative of the origins of the Nation of Israel. In the final chapters of the book of Genesis, Jacob (Israel) and his family took up residence in Egypt, accepting the provision and protection of a covenant relationship with Pharaoh, King of Egypt.[1] In the early chapters of the book of Exodus, a new king arose over Egypt who did not honor the covenant, choosing instead to enslave the Israelites and murder their newborn sons. The Israelites found themselves in a covenant of bondage from which they needed redemption and were unable to redeem themselves.

In the story of The Great Exodus, when God told Moses how He was going to deliver and redeem Israel from Egypt, "Then the Lord said to Moses, 'Now you shall see what I will do to Pharaoh; for under compulsion he will let them go, and under compulsion he will drive them out of his land'" (Exodus 6:1).

When Pharaoh chose to "drive them out of his land" Israel was released from their covenant obligation. At that moment, Israel was divorced from Egypt. The covenant was dissolved, and Israel was free to proceed to the Promised Land with no obligation of allegiance to Egypt.

---

[1] See Appendix for a more complete discussion of this topic as well as on *covenant* and *redemption*, in general.

In fact, the Hebrew words translated here as the phrases *let them go* (*shalach*) and *drive them out* (*garash*) are both translated elsewhere as *divorce* (Malachi 2:16, Leviticus 21:14).

By the manner in which God redeemed Israel from Egypt, He gave new meaning to the word *redemption*. No ransom price was paid, yet the covenant of bondage was dissolved, in a manner that was just. As their redeemer, God justly caused Israel's blood covenant with Egypt to be dissolved, so that Israel was no longer in a covenant of bondage to Egypt.

God brought about the divorce of Israel from Egypt, and God called it *redemption*.

Myth 1 ~
Divorce is Sin

The Myth:

The view that "divorce is sin" is pervasive in the culture of today's church. I have read books by Christian authors, considered experts, written specifically for people who have gone through divorce, which made this very statement, "Divorce is sin." They then followed it up with discussions of forgiveness, moving on, and returning to close fellowship with God. Evidently, these authors felt the need to first make sure the reader, presumably a person who has recently experienced divorce, understands that "divorce is sin."

In today's sermons and Sunday school classes, you won't usually hear this myth expressed quite so bluntly. Most Christians, today, recognizing that many people in our culture have experienced divorce, try to be more sensitive and understanding. Yet, there is often still an unspoken undertone that indicates an assumption of wrong-doing. In some ways, the fact that it is unspoken makes this error even more powerful. Because it is unspoken, the myth is neither challenged nor defended…just assumed correct.

Generally, in defense of this erroneous view (when someone feels compelled to defend it) two primary passages are referenced:

1. Malachi 2:16: "For I hate divorce," says the Lord, the God of Israel…

2. Matthew 19:8-9: He said to them, "Because of your hardness of heart, Moses permitted you to divorce your wives; but from the beginning it has not been this way. And I say to you, whoever divorces his wife, except for immorality, and marries another woman commits adultery."

Scriptural Truth:

I like the sentiment expressed by a dear lady in our church, who experienced divorce many years ago. When someone references Malachi 2:16, she adamantly states, "God doesn't hate it any more than I do!" I know a lot of people who would heartily agree, after having traversed a difficult divorce experience. Just because God says he hates something does not necessarily mean it is sin, though it does denote it as something to be avoided.

Let's look at this passage in context. In Malachi 2:13-16, God is talking about a pervasive issue of the culture at the time Malachi was written, "The Lord has been a witness between you and the wife of your youth, against whom you have dealt treacherously; though she is your companion and your wife by covenant."

The issue was treachery; betrayal of the covenant vows; disregarding a covenant partner whom you have sworn to love, honor, cherish, and protect. Note that there is no rebuke, in this passage, for the wife who was treated treacherously. Both the husband and wife have experienced divorce, but the rebuke is to the party who has dealt treacherously with their spouse. The sin being rebuked is the sin of treachery, not divorce.

In Matthew 19:2-9, Jesus was answering the question asked by the Pharisees, "Is it lawful for a man to divorce his wife *for any cause at all?*"

There is a big difference between the question asked by the Pharisees and the reality of many divorce situations. While it is true that divorce may be the result of one or both parties simply not taking their vows seriously, it is just as common for divorce to be a heart-rending decision made over many sleepless nights, much prayer, and many repeated attempts to resolve major relational issues.

Note, in Matthew 19:9, that Jesus never says that divorce is sin. Rather, he gives a specific example of a circumstance under which divorce is both acceptable and expected.

Simultaneously, He changes the topical focus away from permissibility of divorce to the importance of honoring the marriage covenant and avoiding the sin of adultery. Two specific potential sins are mentioned in this verse. Both are adulterous relationships potentially related to divorce; neither is divorce, itself. Adultery is sin. Divorce is not.

In verse 8, Jesus says that the law that God gave to Moses permits divorce and tells how to go about it, "because of your hardness of heart..." While many Christians, today, understand this to mean that any person who has gone through divorce must have a heart hardened toward God, verse 9 makes it clear that Jesus is referring to the hard heart of one covenant partner toward the other, which may make divorce a necessity.

Note that Jesus never said that the law God gave to Moses was in error or should not have permitted divorce. Rather, God specifically permitted divorce, in the Old Testament Law (Deuteronomy 24:1-4). Where, in all of scripture, has God ever said that sin is permissible? If God said it was permissible and even gave instruction on how to go about it, then it is not sin! Why, then, under Grace, would we presume to impose legalistic rules that are more restrictive than the Old Testament Law?

Many years after the Nation of Israel left Egypt and entered the promised land of Canaan, after many generations of idolatry, repeatedly worshiping the false gods of the Canaanites in total disregard of their sacred covenant oath to worship only the one true God, God said, "And I saw that for all of the adulteries of faithless Israel, *I had sent her away and given her a writ of divorce*, yet her treacherous sister Judah did not fear; but she went and was a harlot also" (Jeremiah 3:8).

God, himself, said that He had divorced Israel, the nation He had once named as His own, by blood covenant. Did He hate that divorce? Of course He did! God loves Israel! It broke His heart to have to divorce her. Yet He did divorce the ten tribes of the northern kingdom of Israel (though not the two tribes of the southern kingdom of Judah who are the ancestors of modern-day Israel), allowing her to be led away into captivity and dispersed among the nations, because of her unfaithfulness. Clearly, nothing that God does can be sin, as the word *sin* is defined as *actions and attitudes that are in opposition to the nature of God.*

In The Great Exodus Story, the Nation of Israel was divorced from the Nation of Egypt. A blood covenant was dissolved. And God was behind it all, orchestrating the whole event, redeeming Israel from their covenant with

Pharaoh, for the purpose of justly liberating them from a covenant which had become abusive bondage. In this sense, and for this purpose, divorce is God's instrument of redemption, used to care for His children!

This does not mean that divorce situations never involve sin, nor does it mean that every divorce is an example of God's redemption, nor that right of redemption extends to all parties involved.

In The Great Exodus Story, Pharaoh clearly sinned against his covenant partners, the Israelites, and Pharaoh's sin clearly led to the divorce. Just as clearly, the divorce itself was brought about by God, as His work of redemption, to justly deliver His chosen nation out of a covenant that had become abusive bondage.

That which was sin for Pharaoh became redemption for Israel, because of God's involvement as redeemer and deliverer on behalf of His people.

Although this model does not apply to all modern instances of divorce of a marriage covenant, it does apply to many.

Our God is a covenant God who desires His children to honor their covenant oaths and covenant obligations. However, God *never* uses covenant as a tool to enslave or abuse, and it is not His desire for His children to be enslaved in a covenant that has become abusive bondage.

Within a covenant, each partner is responsible, before God, for whole-heartedly honoring their own commitments to their covenant partner, for the duration of that covenant. Neither partner is directly responsible for ensuring the longevity of the covenant, itself. Yes, if both partners are fully honoring and living out their covenant vows, then a marriage covenant should endure a lifetime. However, neither party is responsible for the actions of their covenant partner. The focus for each party should be on faithfully and lovingly living out their own covenant vows, not on avoiding divorce, nor on trying to control their covenant partner's behavior.

By focusing on avoiding divorce and erroneously labeling divorce as sin, we actually diminish the sanctity of the marriage covenant.

God holds covenant as sacred, because a well-honored covenant glorifies God by reflecting an important aspect of His nature. However, when a covenant is repeatedly misused as a tool to enslave or abuse, it ceases to reflect God's nature and no longer glorifies Him. At some point, God's redemptive nature is better reflected by the just dissolution of the marriage covenant than by allowing its continued abuse.

Consequences of Perpetuating the Myth:

The erroneous belief that "divorce is sin" can lead to legalism, binding God's children in a law that God did not make…much like the legalism practiced by the Pharisees of Jesus' day, in regard to ceremonial cleanliness and not working (even to heal) on the Sabbath.

This legalistic belief that "divorce is sin" often leads to unnecessary guilt and shame borne by believers who have experienced the pain of a failed marriage…adding insult to injury.

Many believers have experienced divorce as a result of an abusive spouse who repeatedly violated their covenant vows to love, honor, cherish, protect, and forsake all others. These dear children of God, like the Israelites, found themselves in a blood covenant that had become abusive bondage, and from which God has now redeemed them.

To falsely tell them that "divorce is sin" is not only a gross injustice, but also leads to the false perception that God is grossly unjust.

The divorce experience, rather than being rightly viewed as God's loving redemption intervening on behalf of His child to justly deliver them from a covenant of bondage, is viewed, instead, as something evil and wicked which God disapproves of.

As a result, they must either view God as a harsh dictator who wants to see them remain in an abusive relationship, or, in an effort to resolve belief in the myth that "divorce is sin" with the truth that God is love, they must find a way to blame themselves for both the divorce and the abuse. Both of these paths lead toward distancing their relationship with God while fostering unresolved anger and guilt.

Likewise, belief in the myth that "divorce is sin" often leads believers to unnecessarily remain in abusive relationships, because they do not want to "displease God." The combination of ongoing abuse with continued belief in the myth that "divorce is sin" forces them into the same paradigm of misconceptions of God's love and the same unresolved anger and guilt as described in the above paragraph, except further aggravated by lack of relief from the abuse, eventually leading toward either self-loathing or contempt for God, or both, if left unchecked.

As with all forms of legalism, erroneous belief in the myth that "divorce is sin" may also lead to self-righteous attitudes and lack of grace on the part of believers who have not suffered the devastation of a failed marriage. Many times, these holier-than-thou attitudes sneak in unnoticed and remain unaddressed, in the lives of well-meaning God-fearing believers in Christ. How many times have you heard a church member smugly whisper, when the child of a single parent misbehaves, "Well, they're from a broken home, you know!" as though that one fact sums up all there is to be said on the root of the child's misbehavior…and as though children of Christian married couples never misbehave?

Moving Forward Past the Myth:

Since you are reading this book, it is likely that you may be a believer in Christ who has experienced divorce. I know nothing of the circumstances of your divorce situation, nor of anything that may have occurred in your marital relationship prior to the divorce.

You may be guilty of breaking your covenant vows prior to the divorce, either of committing adultery, or in some other way of failing to love, honor, cherish and protect the person who was your spouse. You may be guilty of the adulterous scenario mentioned by Jesus in Matthew 19:9, of divorcing your spouse, with the specific intent of marrying another, or of otherwise using the divorce as an opportunity to defraud your spouse.

If you did break your covenant vows in that marriage or otherwise treated your spouse unjustly during the divorce, and you have not dealt with those issues, then you need to spend time in prayer, asking God what to do. God offers forgiveness for sin. He may ask you to also seek forgiveness of the person whom you sinned against, or to somehow seek to make restitution (Matthew 5:23-24). However, if that is the case, the issue to be dealt with is whatever way you broke your covenant vows or behaved unjustly, not the divorce, itself. The divorce, itself, was not sin, but rather the result of sin, and focusing on the divorce would only dilute your effectiveness in dealing with the real issue of your broken vows.

If you are one of the many believers who did not break your covenant vows, who did all you could to honor your marriage and demonstrate love to your partner, yet have experienced divorce, then you are not guilty of sin in regard to the divorce. You almost certainly made mistakes, as everyone does. However, honest mistakes are not the same thing as breaking covenant vows.

If this is your case, and you have been carrying unnecessary guilt, feeling that you are somehow responsible, that you should have been able to somehow prevent the divorce, then it is time to let it go. Recognize that there are many things in life over which we have no control, accept the situation for what it is, and thank God for His loving redemption from what was, apparently, an extremely difficult marital relationship.

Praise God, for His wonderful redemption!

I am so thankful that our Heavenly Father does not see us as being guilty of committing a great sin, but rather as having been lovingly redeemed by His "outstretched arm" (Exodus 6:6)!

Myth 2 ~

You Have Missed God's Best Plan for Your Life (if you have ever been through a divorce)

The Myth:

The American "dream," perhaps the human "dream," is to grow up, marry, raise kids, enjoy relationships with family, and grow old together.

Reading the Genesis story of life in the Garden of Eden, it is easy to see the source of this dream. It is a godly desire, placed in human hearts by God himself, and it is how things were before the fall of man.

Unfortunately, sin entered the world, bringing with it the consequences of sin. Life, today, frequently deviates from the vision we aspire to, starting out in life.

For those who lose a spouse to death, the event is seen by the church (and society as a whole) as something beyond their control. Therefore, it must be God ordained. Their life has deviated from the human dream, but is assumed to be still under God's control and plan for their life.

Divorce, on the other hand, is seen as something which we should have been able to control. Either we should have been able to prevent the divorce and reconcile to the marriage partner, or we should have been able to foresee the potential relational issues and not have married that person to begin with. Depending on the person and circumstances, one of two assumptions is made about the individual who has gone through divorce:

1. Either, the divorce, itself, is viewed as a sinful act, which they should have prevented, or

2. The marriage is assumed to have been based on a selfish rebellious act, in which they failed to seek God. Had they sought God's wisdom in choosing a marriage partner, God would have blessed the marriage, and, presumably, the marriage would not have ended in divorce.

Either way, the person who experienced divorce is now viewed as someone who has missed God's perfect plan for their life, and must now settle for God's second-best plan.

Biblical Truth:

With God, there is no Plan B. God is in control, start to finish. If you are a believer in Christ, then you were chosen "…in Him before the foundation of the world, that we should be holy and blameless before Him. In love He predestined us to adoption as sons through Jesus Christ to Himself, according to the kind intention of His will to the praise of the glory of His grace, which He freely bestowed on us His beloved" (Ephesians 1:4-6).

The Bible tells of many great men of God, who went through a period where it appeared, from a human perspective, like their lives were off track from God's plan. Yet God showed it all to be a part of His plan.

Abraham lived 99 years with no heir, and pitched a tent his whole life on land he did not own, although God himself had promised Abraham a vast land ownership as an inheritance for his multitude of descendants.

Jacob, the trickster, fled home in fear of his life, served his father-in-law for many years, then fled from his father-in-law, before returning to the land of his birth and his promised inheritance, where God gave him the name Israel.

Joseph was enslaved and imprisoned for much of his adult life, before seeing the fulfillment of the visions God had given him as a child, attaining a position with authority and ability to rescue his family from starvation.

Moses, after committing murder, fled to live in another land for 40 years, before returning to Egypt to lead the Israelites out of bondage.

The list goes on...and in each case, by the end of the story, it is clear that God was in control, from start to finish.

Now, let's look again at The Great Exodus Story. The book of Exodus opens with "Now a new king arose over Egypt, who did not know Joseph" (Exodus 1:8). The blood covenant cut between Pharaoh and Joseph has been neglected and forgotten, and the heir to that covenant, the new Pharaoh, rather than honoring the covenant with his sworn blood-brothers, the Israelites, chooses, instead, to enslave them and to kill their sons. God intervenes to redeem them "with an outstretched arm and with great judgments" (Exodus 6:6).

So, has Israel missed God's perfect plan? They find themselves in a blood covenant which has become bondage and from which they need redemption. Did they fail to seek God's wisdom before entering into covenant with Pharaoh? Did they fail to honor their covenant with Pharaoh and thus cause the relational deterioration which led to divorce?

Not at all! It was all foreordained of God, all part of God's perfect plan for Israel, and all prophesied in advance to Abraham. In Genesis 15:13-14, God told Abraham what would happen to his descendants and for how long. It was all part of God's plan!

Here is an example of a blood covenant being entered into, lasting 430 years, then ending in divorce, all of which was foreordained of God and part of God's perfect plan for His people. God intended for Israel to enter into covenant with Egypt. God knew that they would be enslaved. God himself redeemed them from that covenant of bondage and delivered them through the divorce.

Consequences of Perpetuating the Myth:

Too often, people who have been through divorce are treated as second-class citizens in the church family, as people who simply cannot be trusted to have the wisdom required for a leadership position. We are too often seen as having failed a great trust and, as a consequence, no longer to be trusted.

Worse, we believers who have been through divorce often see ourselves the same way. We are prone to see ourselves as having made a horrible mistake which has taken our life off-track, and now the best we can hope for is a few mercy drops of God's blessing, crumbs from the children's table, as we work out the second-best life we can manage.

The myth of "missing God's best plan" conceals the truth that, if you are a believer in Christ who is trusting and following the guidance of the Holy Spirit, then you are God's chosen child, directly on track for all of God's bountiful blessings which He has stored up for you, and all of the richness of the destiny He has foreordained for you, before the foundation of the world. You are exactly where God wants you to be, and your life experiences are precisely as He orchestrated them to be for the purpose of blessing you with your specific destiny and inheritance!

Moving Forward Past the Myth:

We all have certain visions and expectations of life. Those visions and expectations are seldom greater than at the moment we take our marriage vows. Seldom are those visions so thoroughly shattered as during a divorce.

So, how do we move past the shattered dreams?

It is not an easy process and it does not happen overnight. The first step, though, is to recognize that, no matter how out of control your life may feel, if you are a believer in Christ, then your life is still in His control and under His direction.

Your divorce did not catch God by surprise. God knew, before the wedding ever took place, how and when your marriage would end. More importantly, He also knows exactly how He is going to use that experience to lead you into the destiny that He preordained for you before the foundation of the world.

Accept God's destiny for your life and recognize His sovereignty over your life. Spend much time in prayer, asking the Holy Spirit to use this experience of shattered dreams to shine His glory through your life, and to further transform your heart to the image of Christ. If there are sins related to your previous marriage that need to be dealt with, then prayerfully address those.

Then start seeking God's revelation of His vision for your life. We can trust that God's vision for our lives is always greater than our own. Stop trying to convince God to get on board with your vision for your life (as we are all prone to do, at times). Start seeking God's vision for your life and ask Him to make it your vision.

God probably won't lay out your entire life plan for you in advance (though I have often caught myself praying that He would). However, if you prayerfully seek His heart, He will begin to grow a new vision within your heart and to show you the next step you should take.

Walk in what vision God gives you as you continue to seek a clearer vision. He usually shows us one step at a time. Expect to have to take each step in faith, before the next step is revealed.

Trust God to know His plan for your life and your destiny...and to know how best to reveal it to you!

Myth 3 ~

Divorce is Always the Fault of Both Parties

The Myth:

Relational communication requires hard work from both parties. Communication issues are, in most instances, at least partially contributed to by both parties. Therefore, it is assumed that divorce is the result of poor communication, which must be at least partially the fault of both parties.

This view conveniently reinforces the myth that divorce is sin. If both parties are at fault then both parties can be in sin. If it were possible for a divorce to be the fault of only one party, then the other party would not be responsible for the divorce, which would contradict the thesis that divorce is sin.

In my experience, I have never heard anyone even attempt to provide biblical support in defense of this myth. It is simply an assumption based on the myth that divorce is sin, combined with the assumption that divorce is the result of communication issues, at which no human is perfect.

Despite the lack of any biblical defense, this myth has very strong support within today's church. It is an opinion that is often extolled by well-meaning friends giving advice to people facing divorce or emerging from divorce. It is also often repeated by people who have experienced divorce, either to blame the other person for the consequences of their own actions (inappropriately shifting blame), or to take on personal responsibility for actions and circumstances beyond their control (inappropriately carrying blame).

Biblical Truth:

The assumption that all divorces are a result of poor communication is simply a false assumption. While it is true that miscommunication often contributes to issues that may lead toward divorce, this is not always the case. It is all too common for one partner to simply decide to break their covenant vows; to "deal treacherously" with their spouse (Malachi 2:14-16) or to leave their spouse for the purpose of marrying another (Matthew 19:9).

While it is true that, as humans, we are all imperfect and all make mistakes, this does not mean that we all break our covenant vows.

The assertion that a divorce is always the fault of both parties fails to recognize some fundamental truths about relationships.

1. To have a strong successful marriage requires a lot of work and a lot of self-sacrifice by both parties.

2. One person cannot have enough commitment for two. A yoke of oxen can only pull the load if they work together. It only takes one running the wrong direction, or lying down, to wreck the whole cart.

3. If one partner decides to dishonor their marriage covenant, there is absolutely nothing the other partner can do to prevent it from happening.

Now, let's look at a couple of examples from the Bible:

1. In The Great Exodus, Pharaoh broke his covenant vows to Israel, enslaving them and murdering their children. Israel had done nothing to cause this issue. God redeemed Israel, condemned Pharaoh, and never gave any indication that Israel had done anything wrong. God arranged for Israel to be divorced from Egypt, dissolving the covenant between them.

2. In Genesis, Adam and Eve were created in covenant with God. They violated that covenant and, as a result of their sin, many of Adam and Eve's descendants will be condemned to an eternity in Hell, eternally divorced from the God with whom they were originally created to be in covenant. If we accept as truth the assertion that divorce is always the fault of both parties, then we would have to conclude that Adam and Eve's original sin and the resulting condemnation to Hell of many of their descendants is as much God's fault as Adam and Eve's. Since this is clearly not the case, the thesis is proven false...a myth.

Consequences of Perpetuating the Myth:

There certainly are many instances of divorce rooted in miscommunication or "irreconcilable differences". For those instances, it is probably not particularly beneficial or healthy to be overly concerned about who was more at fault, and it makes a lot more sense to just say, "We both could have done more," and leave it at that.

However, there are many other instances where one party has repeatedly violated the covenant with no sign of repentance or commitment to change, while the other partner has gone above-and-beyond the call of duty, in an effort to do everything possible to resolve differences. In these instances, it is particularly hurtful for the partner who has completely invested themselves in the marriage relationship to be told by well-meaning friends that the divorce is as much their fault as the other party's. In these instances, propagation of this myth can lead to:

1. Inappropriate and unnecessary guilt on the part of innocent victims of broken covenants.

2. Redirection of guilt and self-justification on the part of persons guilty of breaking their covenant vows, "Well, you know, it takes two!" (which would be a true statement if used in the context of what it takes to build a healthy marital relationship, but is completely false when used in the context of what it takes to destroy a relationship).

3. Believers staying unnecessarily in abusive relationships, because they do not want to "displease God," and feel that the situation is somehow their fault, or that it is up to them to make the marriage work, even without their spouse's support or commitment.

Fundamentally, propagation of the myth that "divorce is always the fault of both parties" minimalizes intentional unrepentant covenant-breaking sins against a marriage partner while elevating minor unintentional mistakes and well-intended miscommunications. The result is that the actions of the partner who is guilty of "dealing treacherously" against their spouse are erroneously justified, while the actions of the partner who has honestly put forth their best effort in giving sacrificially of themself are erroneously condemned, in a vain attempt to unjustly force both onto an equal level of shared responsibility.

Thank God, we do not need to justify ourselves in the sight of men, because God knows our hearts (Acts 15:8, 2 Chronicles 6:30)!

Moving Forward Past the Myth:

Divorce seems to leave us second-guessing ourselves far more than most life experiences. As believers in Christ who have been taught to honor our covenants, we entered into matrimony fully expecting to be married to this person for the rest of our lives. We took our solemn vows with full intent of living out those vows for the rest of our lives, and fully believing we had all the resources available to ensure that happened. Yet, somehow, something went bad wrong...then spiraled to worse...and despite our best intentions and efforts the marriage ended in divorce.

We are left with a head full of questions and not many answers, "What went wrong? What more could I have done to prevent the divorce? What more could I have done to strengthen the relationship? Did I just choose the wrong person to marry? I thought I prayed and received an answer from God before marrying; did I fail to hear God? Do I even know God's voice when I hear it?" We can torture ourselves with these questions for as long as we choose to.

So, choose to stop...now.

Maybe the divorce was the direct result of your sin against your spouse, in breaking your marriage vows, or otherwise defrauding your spouse. If that is the case, ask forgiveness if you haven't already; seek the guidance of the Holy Spirit in what you can do to make restitution to the person you wronged; then let it go and move on. Do not continue to carry guilt for what God has forgiven.

Maybe the divorce was due to circumstances beyond your control, with your having done nothing to break your covenant vows. If that is the case, then don't continue to blame yourself for circumstances beyond your control.

The issue of carrying blame, feeling responsible, and trying to figure out what went wrong often seems to be more troubling for a partner who has done all they could to fully invest themselves in the marriage, than for one who has broken their covenant vows. Someone who has sinned against their partner usually knows what they did wrong, and understands the cause and effect. However, those who have done nothing wrong, yet continue to feel equally responsible for the failure of the marriage, are stuck with trying to figure out in what way they failed and how to ensure it doesn't happen again in another relationship. In a very real sense, the innocent party feels compelled to try to find something to blame on themself, in order to have something to repent of.

If this describes your current situation, then I recommend, from personal experience, that you spend some time praying The Serenity Prayer, by theologian Reinhold Niebuhr, with special emphasis on the part about the need for wisdom:

The Serenity Prayer

God, grant me the serenity to accept the things I cannot change;

Courage to change the things I can;

And wisdom to know the difference.

Life is full of things over which we have no control. Do not continue beating yourself up, or feeling responsible, for something you did not do. Give it to God, trusting Him to be in control long after the realization that you are not.

Myth 4 ~

Divorce is a Perpetual State of Being
(once divorced, eternally marked as a divorcee)

The Myth:

Every time we fill out a census form or a job application, we're asked our marital status, and given choices of Single, Married, Divorced or Widowed. An individual who went through a divorce many years ago, and has not married again feels compelled to label themselves, "Divorced."

Within the church, we often add yet another marital status, "Divorced and Remarried."

As though it is not enough that a person has gone through the devastating experience of a failed marriage, as though it is not enough to tell them the divorce was their fault, that they should have prevented it, and that it is sinful, we go one more step to forever label them as "divorced," a stigmatic label that is never removed no matter what further life accomplishments may be achieved, or how successful and enriching a later marriage may become.

Biblical Truth:

~ My covenant relationships define who I am...my identity ~

What's in a name?

For several years, Dr. Laura Schlessinger has hosted a radio talk show in which she dispenses advice on relationships, particularly on parenting. In years past, callers to the show used to always introduced themselves as, "Hello, Dr. Laura, my name is John Doe and I am the father of my children." The basis for the odd-sounding introduction was a biblical truth that Dr. Laura referenced. Who I am, I am in my covenant relationships. From a biblical perspective, our covenant relationships define who we are.

When God made a covenant with Abram, Abram received a new name, Abraham (Genesis 17:1-5). Likewise Sarai received a new name, Sarah (Genesis 17:15). The new names signify that Abraham and Sarah are no longer the same people they were prior to the covenant. They now have a covenant partner, and that covenant relationship has redefined who they are. Their identities have been changed.

We see this as a common practice throughout the Bible. When Pharaoh made a covenant with Joseph, he gave Joseph a new name, "Zaphenath-Paneah" (Genesis 41:45). When Daniel and his three Hebrew friends were adopted into the household of Nebuchadnezzar, king of Babylon, they were all given new names (Daniel 1:7). Even today, when a man and woman are married, it is customary for the woman to take her husband's last name as her own, signifying that her identity has changed, with a new character trait defined by her new covenant relationship.

Even God introduced himself to Moses in the Sinai desert as, "I Am Who I Am... I am the God of your fathers, the

God of Abraham, the God of Isaac, and the God of Jacob… This is My name forever, and this is My memorial-name to all generations" (Exodus 3:14-15). God, Himself, omnipotent creator of the universe, introduced Himself in terms of His covenant relationships.

I am who I am:

In biblical language, we seldom read a sentence starting with "I am…" followed by anything temporary or transitory. "I am…" statements are almost invariably followed by a defining characteristic of that person, or by reference to a covenant relationship, such as "I am the Bread of Life" (John 6:35) or "I am the Light of the World" (John 8:12).

In contrast, consider Jesus' statement on the cross, "I thirst" (John 19:28 *NKJV*). Note that He did not say, "I am thirsty," as would be more typical today. The state of thirst is temporary and does not define who Jesus is.

My wife, Sherri, pretends annoyance at me for saying things like, "I thirst," "I hunger," or "I grow weary." She says I sound like I think I'm Jesus. I say it this way partly out of fun (yes, I have a bizarre sense of humor) because I realize how odd it sounds in our culture, but also because it makes a point that those are temporary conditions that do not define who I am. Who I am is God's child, Sherri's husband, and my children's father.

My identity cannot be defined by a covenant that does not exist:

Divorce does not define who I am, as implied by a statement such as, "I am divorced." Divorce is an experience I have been through, not a definition of who I am.

Likewise, divorce is not a perpetual state of being. I have been through divorce, I am not in divorce.

Saying that I am divorced would be like saying Jesus is dead. Jesus died, but He is not dead. Death was an experience He passed through before emerging very much alive, on the other side. Likewise, divorce is an experience I have passed through, before emerging very much redeemed from that covenant, on the other side. I went through a divorce, but I am not divorced. Divorce is *not* a state that I continue to live in.

Since my covenant relationships define my identity, who I am, the moment the divorce was complete and I was no longer in covenant with Marie, that covenant ceased to exist and ceased to define who I am. I do not describe myself as divorced, nor do I refer to Marie as my ex-wife. That covenant relationship is not simply altered; it no longer exists. Therefore, it neither defines who I am, nor who Marie is.

Lesson from The Great Exodus:

When Israel left Egypt, they were no longer Egyptian slaves. Instead, they had become Israel, God's Chosen People.

However, it took Israel 40 years to adjust their thinking, to stop defining themselves as Egyptian slaves. When obstacles were encountered, they instinctively wished for Pharaoh to protect and provide for them. They had so associated themselves with Pharaoh and Pharaoh's provision and protection, that they forgot the pain, hardships, slavery, and murder of their sons, and longed for Pharaoh to provide them with food, shelter and protection.

Only a few Israelites of that generation, including Moses, Joshua and Caleb, were able to see themselves as God saw them: Redeemed from their covenant of bondage to Pharaoh. Delivered from their slavery in Egypt. Free to embrace their new covenant with God and to be led by Him into their inheritance and destiny.

Consequences of Perpetuating the Myth:

When we define ourselves as "divorced," we limit our potential, hanging onto old wounds and failed relationships. There are *not* multiple marital statuses! We are either married or single. I am either in a marriage covenant or not in a marriage covenant. Once a covenant has ended, once I have been redeemed from a covenant of bondage, that covenant no longer exists and ceases to define who I am.

When people from our church family continue to call us "divorced" or "divorced and remarried," they are, because of the other myths previously discussed, continuing to label us by what is commonly (though erroneously) believed to be sin. They are affixing a label of "sinner" and "untrustworthy" that is never removed and never lived down. This is completely contrary to Christ, the Christian faith, and all that Christ did on the cross! Even if sin was involved (which is not necessarily the case) why would we continue to define a person by their past sin?

This brings us to a related topic, slightly tangential to the current topic. For similar reasons, I do not like referring to Christians as "sinners saved by grace." Yes, I was formerly a sinner, but I am no longer. Although I do not claim to be sinless, sin no longer defines my identity. Since entering into covenant with God through Jesus Christ, I am now a child of God. My identity is no longer defined by that old covenant with the kingdom of darkness. I have been redeemed from that covenant, divorced from sin and death, and no longer defined by it. It may be who I once was, but it is *not* who I am!

If I continue to think of myself as a sinner, rather than as a holy child of God, then I, like the Israelites in the wilderness, will continue to turn to the comfort and protection of sin when I am scared or hurt, rather than turning to the Lord God, my Father, "draw[ing] near to the throne of grace, so that [I] may receive mercy and find grace to help in time of need" (Hebrews 4:16).

Moving Forward Past the Myth:

While we cannot change how others see us, or how others refer to us, we can change how we see ourselves. More importantly, we can change our understanding of how God sees us.

Spend a little time each day in prayer and Bible reading, specifically asking God to show you how He sees you, and to help you to see yourself through His eyes. God sees you through the eyes of a parent who loves His Child, with all His heart.

God does not see you as "divorced." He sees you as possessing the valuable life experience of having lived through a divorce, and He intends for that life experience to become a useful tool in the ministry for which He has ordained and destined you.

Myth 5 ~

Remarriage is Sin
(an adulterous relationship)

The Myth:

There are two sources of this view. The first comes from the Roman Catholic Church view of divorce, which is shared by some of the more traditional Protestant Churches. As I understand it, the official position of the Roman Catholic Church simply does not recognize divorce as valid. Therefore, since divorce is not recognized as valid, the two original marriage partners are viewed as still married, and if either partner remarries, the second marriage is viewed as an invalid, illegal, adulterous relationship.

The second source of this view is pulled from a few scriptures, with the primary reference of Matthew 19:8-9, "He said to them, 'Because of your hardness of heart, Moses permitted you to divorce your wives; but from the beginning it has not been this way. And I say to you, whoever divorces his wife, except for immorality, and marries another woman commits adultery.'"

Biblical Truth:

If we are going to take a legalistic view of the topic (and this myth is nothing if not legalistic) then let's check to see what was actually said in The Law.

Deuteronomy 24:1-4 clearly permits divorce, clearly requires the issuance of a certificate of divorce, and clearly allows remarriage after divorce. In fact, the whole purpose of the certificate of divorce was for proof of no longer being married and therefore available for remarriage.

The only prohibition in this passage of Deuteronomy is that the former husband may not take the woman back as his wife after she has been married to another man. Interestingly, the Roman Catholic Church would take a view diametrically opposed to The Law recorded in Deuteronomy, and would say that both the divorce and the second marriage were invalid and the original husband should take the woman back as his wife.

Isn't it interesting how legalistic we can be while completely ignoring The Law?

Now, let's look at the passage in Matthew 19, remembering that Jesus was answering a legal question presented by the Pharisees in an attempt to trap Him. The question was, "Is it lawful for a man to divorce his wife for any cause at all?" Jesus is not answering whether or not divorce is in some instances permissible and justified, or whether remarriage after divorce is permissible. He is answering whether a man can lawfully divorce his wife *for any cause at all*...because she burned his toast that morning...or, more specifically, because he found another woman he likes better. Jesus is saying that if a man divorces his wife for the purpose of marrying another woman, that he is as guilty of adultery as if he had not first divorced her. As always, Jesus is judging the heart of the matter, rather than the legalistic loopholes.

Just as in the Sermon on the Mount, where Jesus tells us "...everyone who looks at a woman with lust for her has already committed adultery with her in his heart" (Matthew 5:28) and "...everyone who is angry with his brother shall be guilty [of murder] before the court" (Matthew 5:22), His goal is *not* to add another layer of legalistic rules we cannot hope to attain, so as to make us feel a deeper level of guilt. Rather, in speaking to an audience who are experts in God's law without understanding God's heart, Jesus is demonstrating that we can never attain righteousness by strict adherence to legalistic rules, nor can we escape guilt through legalistic loopholes. His whole point is that legalism will never achieve the intended goal, because the sin problem runs too deep. The problem is with the sin nature that is in our hearts, which can only be overcome by God giving us a new nature.

Christ did not come with the intent of giving us a stricter set of legalistic rules than that given to Moses in the Old Testament Law. Rather, He came to free us from legalism, by giving us a new nature, through entering into a new covenant with the Father. He came to redeem us from Adam's covenant with the kingdom of darkness, so that through that divorce from our sin nature, we might enter a new covenant with the Father, in which we could be indwelt and led by His Holy Spirit.

For a specific example of God blessing a marriage of someone with a prior history of union, consider the woman named Rahab, who hid the Israelite spies in Jericho (Joshua 2:1-3). Rahab was a harlot. Her occupation was prostitution. Rahab made her living by having sexual intercourse with men, in exchange for money. Yet, because of her faith, she was protected when Jericho was defeated (Joshua 6:23-25) and later married an Israelite named Salmon. Not only did God not object to the marriage, but he blessed and endorsed it, choosing Rahab to become the great-great-grandmother of King David, and the direct ancestor of Jesus Christ! The first chapter of the first book of the New Testament opens with a listing of the genealogy of Jesus Christ, in which Rahab is prominently listed in Matthew 1:5.

When God redeems you, you are redeemed! That old covenant of bondage is gone, dissolved, and you are completely free from its previous obligations and limitations!

Consequences of Perpetuating the Myth:

Like the erroneous belief that "divorce is sin", the erroneous belief that "remarriage is sin" leads to legalism, unnecessarily binding God's children in a law that God did not make.

In the Garden of Eden, God told Adam not to eat of the fruit of the tree of the knowledge of good and evil (Genesis 2:17). Later, when Eve was tempted by the serpent, she (or Adam) had added to God's law. God had warned Adam not to eat of that one tree. Eve misquoted God as saying, "You shall not eat from it *or touch it*, or you will die" (Genesis 3:3).

Adding to what God said, to make the rule more restrictive than God intended, did not protect Eve from violating God's command. If anything, the unnecessary additional restrictiveness may have led toward her rebellious decision to disobey God.

How many times do we drive people from the church because of our own false legalistic attitudes? How many Christian married couples avoid church, because they have been told they are living in sin and can never be legally wed in holy matrimony, because one of them has previously been through a divorce?

I have personally encountered several couples who love God and faithfully attend church, but experience either intense guilt or frustrated confusion, because they have been led to believe their marriage is unacceptable to God, due to one of them having previously experienced divorce.

No good ever comes of adding legalistic restrictions beyond what God has given us. That path leads only toward unnecessary guilt and bondage.

Christ leads us to freedom through redemption!

Moving Forward Past the Myth:

Maybe you have already remarried since your divorce. If you have, and if that has been a source of guilt, confusion, anger, or relational distance, then let it all go. Spend some time in prayerful Bible study, starting with the scriptures referenced in this book. Don't take my word for it - study the Bible for yourself. Learn God's heart toward you, your current spouse, and your marriage.

It is hard to draw close to someone that you believe resents or dislikes a covenant relationship that is very dear to your heart. You are not likely to draw closer to God until you resolve your perception of His view of your current marriage. Study the scriptures and see for yourself that God does not resent you having married again after divorce. God is not holding you to sacred vows sworn in a covenant that no longer exists, nor does He see you as in a state of perpetual sin.

If you did divorce with the specific intent of marrying another, then you did sin against the person who was formerly your spouse, and you need to deal with that sin, if you haven't already. So deal with it, prayerfully. Once dealt with, accept God's forgiveness and move on.

If you have not remarried since your divorce, then don't worry about it. Seek God's plans for your life, right now, as a single believer. Realize that being single does have advantages and does open unique ministry opportunities. Embrace this as a time, not only of unique ministry opportunity, but also of healing and learning more about yourself. Walk in the guidance of the Holy Spirit. If, at some point, God leads you toward marriage, great! If not, equally great!

Myth 6 ~

A Church Leadership Role is Forbidden
(for anyone who has ever experienced divorce)

The Myth:

The erroneous view that "a church leadership role is forbidden for anyone who has ever experienced divorce," is also pervasive in today's church. To a large extent, it goes hand-in-hand with the other myths we have previously discussed. If we (erroneously) assume that divorce is sin, that divorce is always the fault of both parties, that a person who has experienced divorce has missed God's best plan for their life and is forever labeled "divorced," and that a second marriage is an invalid adulterous relationship, then it is very easy to conclude that such a person should never hold a position of leadership in the church.

The biblical reference used to defend this myth comes from the Apostle Paul's letters to the church, starting with 1 Timothy 3:2, "An overseer, then, must be above reproach, the husband of one wife, temperate, prudent, respectable, hospitable, able to teach…" and similar passages from other epistles written by the Apostle Paul.

Defenders of this myth interpret "husband of one wife" to mean the man cannot have remarried after experiencing a divorce. In other words, they are holding the biblically unsubstantiated view of the Roman Catholic Church, that the divorce is not valid and, therefore, that the second marriage is a bigamous relationship.

Biblical Truth:

As already demonstrated in the previous chapters, divorce is not sin and is valid, and it is permissible for someone who has been through divorce to remarry. Therefore, the second marriage is valid and is not bigamous.

I have been through divorce. I have married again. I am married to one woman, my wife, Sherri. Therefore, the phrase "husband of one wife" includes me, as well as others in similar circumstances.

In the first century, however, polygamy was relatively common, especially among the gentile nations to whom the Apostle Paul was writing. At that time, and in those cultures, it was not unusual for a man to be simultaneously married to multiple wives. As might be expected, these polygamous relationships often led to dissension and jealousy within the home. Therefore, the caution that a church elder should be "the husband of one wife" makes perfect sense in light of the culture to whom it was written.

Most Bible commentators indicate that the phrase "husband of one wife" might be better interpreted as "man of one woman," and is intended to address the importance of a husband's fidelity to his wife. In context of the overall passage, this interpretation really makes the most sense, and is certainly the most pertinent, today.

In either case, the overall emphasis of this passage (as well as other similar passages) is on the need for a leader in the church to be above reproach, to be responsible, to be a good manager, to be of good reputation, etc., and has nothing at all to do with prior marital statuses.

For a specific biblical example to illustrate the absurdity of the all-too-common misinterpretation that the criteria "husband of one wife" means "a church leadership role is forbidden for anyone who has ever experienced divorce," one need look no further than the life of the Apostle Paul, himself, as recorded in the book of Acts.

Paul, prior to his conversion to Christianity, had been a zealous persecutor of the Christian faith. He had stood by, approvingly, as Stephen, the first Christian martyr, was stoned to death (Acts 22:20). Paul (then known as Saul) personally pursued believers in Christ, for the specific purpose of seeing them thrown in prison and possibly put to death (Acts 8:3 and 9:1-2).

After his conversion to Christianity, Paul was, understandably, treated with suspicion by the church leaders, in Jerusalem. They were concerned that Paul's claim of a conversion experience might be simply a trick to learn more about the church, for the purpose of continued persecution. Yet, they did accept Paul, after much urging and prompting by Barnabas (Acts 9:26-30), and Paul eventually became both an apostle of the church and one of the most effective Christian missionaries of all time, not to mention the most prolific author of the New Testament.

If there was anyone who should rightfully have been permanently excluded from consideration for a church leadership position, it was Paul.

Paul, himself, said, "For I am the least of the apostles, and not fit to be called an apostle, because I persecuted the church of God" (1 Corinthians 15:9).

So, Paul, prior persecutor of the church, responsible for the imprisonment and death of many Christians, became not only a church elder, but an apostle of the church.

Would the Apostle Paul, being so very aware of his own prior guilt and his own lack of fitness to be called an apostle, instruct the church to disqualify someone from ever holding a church leadership position on the basis that they had remarried sometime after a previous divorce experience? Would Paul, who became an apostle after having committed crimes against the church and having encouraged the murder of Christians, require that someone with no known violation of God's law be excluded from church leadership because of something that had happened in their past, a divorce over which they may or may not have had control, and which was completely within the boundaries of God's law, as recorded in the Old Testament?

Clearly, the answer is no! Clearly, this all-too-common interpretation is, in fact, a *misinterpretation*…a myth.

Consequences of Perpetuating the Myth:

In general, given the pervasiveness of this viewpoint, I think most people who have been through divorce would just as soon not stir up potential dissension by challenging this myth in an effort to become a church deacon.

However, I do believe that churches often miss opportunities for some very good potential leaders by choosing to overlook anyone who has ever experienced divorce. Moreover, they inherently miss an opportunity to have someone in a leadership role who can identify with those who have experienced divorce.

The worst consequence of this myth, though, is that it leads directly to the continuation of stigmatic labeling and self-righteous legalism. If we are (falsely) convinced that no one who has ever been through divorce should ever hold a church leadership position, then it becomes imperative to always keep track of everyone's prior marital statuses, and to judge their competence as a function of those prior statuses.

When the church counsel or nominating committee meets to discuss potential candidates for deacons or elders, they feel compelled to exclude anyone who has ever experienced divorce. "What about John Doe?" proposes one deacon, "He's a godly man with sound judgment, biblical understanding, and a heart for ministry. John would make an excellent deacon!" "Oh, no!" replies another, "Don't you remember? John's first wife divorced him and ran off with the postman, 30 years ago. John and Jane have been married for nearly 20 years, now, and raised their four kids, together. John isn't qualified to be a deacon!"

See how one false belief feeds and reinforces another in a vicious cycle of false condemnation?

Isn't it wonderful to know that our Heavenly Father, who is not blinded by false perceptions and myths, does not condemn us? Rather, He has redeemed us to a life of freedom to love and honor Him!

Moving Forward Past the Myth:

Perhaps the leadership at the church you attend correctly interprets the various passages in the New Testament epistles regarding the qualifications of a church elder, and has taken a strong stand to not let prior marital statuses be a determining factor in selection of deacons or elders. If so, count yourself blessed!

For a large number of churches, this is an on-going issue that is routinely considered in the selection of deacons or elders. In some cases it is a matter of the church leadership misinterpreting the referenced passages and developing an official policy, accordingly. In other cases, the church leadership understands the correct interpretation, but are concerned about how the congregation might view the situation, and choose to err on the politically conservative side. "So long as we have plenty of qualified men who have not been through divorce and are willing to serve," the unofficial position logics, "why stir up potential conflict by placing someone who has been through divorce in a leadership position?"

We are not likely to see attitudes of others within the church changed very quickly, nor would it likely be constructive to stir up unnecessary dissension by challenging your church on leadership selection policies.

However, this is only an issue if it is a high priority for you to be in an official leadership position, in your church. For me, personally, it has simply become a non-issue. Although I may not agree with the policy, I feel no compelling need to be ordained a deacon. So, I have simply found other avenues of ministry.

My advice is, don't sweat it! "Accept the things you cannot change," unless the Holy Spirit specifically leads you to lovingly strive for changes in policy. Recognize that you do not need man's approval to be a minister of the gospel. Ask God, and He will open ministry opportunities for you.

In some ways, it is sort of freeing, really. Once you recognize you're not likely to have man's approval in an official church-ordained leadership position, that frees you to pursue whatever ministry God may lead you to, without worrying about the approval of others.

As an example, while I do not know in what ways God may choose to use this book you are reading, I am writing it in faith, believing that He will use it to especially minister to believers who have experienced divorce. It is a rather unconventional book, expressing a view that some may see as controversial. While it is not my intent to be controversial, it is my intent to expose error in some views that are commonly accepted by many to be truth.

I wonder…if I had not personally experienced divorce and if I were an ordained church deacon with full approval of the entire church membership, would I have either the insight to recognize the need or the courage to write this book? As much as I would like to think I would, I likely would not.

And that's okay, too. I am more than happy to be used of God in ways that others, with different life experiences, would probably not be used!

Myth 7 ~
Wasted Years, Effort, and Emotions

The Myth:

This myth is less about how the church, in general, sees divorce, and more about how believers who have experienced divorce tend to see ourselves, and our own lives.

Most of us, while we are married, invest an incredible amount of emotional energy into that marital relationship. For those of us who go through intensely difficult marriages while still trying to resolve issues, there is an even deeper level of investment. Putting your whole heart into trying to explore and resolve major relational issues requires an incredible amount of energy and emotional investment.

The result is that, by the time the marriage finally does end in divorce, years have passed, and those years have been spent with our lives largely centered around working to build up a failing relationship. We emerge through the divorce to realize that we are now 5, 10, 15 or 20 years older than when we started down the path of matrimony, that we are now emotionally drained, and that we're not too sure we ever want to invest that much of ourselves into any relationship ever again.

At the same time, we still hold a remnant of the human dream. After all, if we did not treasure the ideal of mutually having, holding, honoring and cherishing a marriage partner with whom we grow old together, we would not have invested so much of ourselves for so long.

So we find ourselves, a few months or years after the divorce, grieving the lost dream. By this point we're no longer grieving the failed marriage. We realize that the marriage would never have worked and had to end, and we are thankful it is over. Yet, we grieve the wasted years, wasted effort, wasted emotional investment that resulted in...*divorce*. It feels like such an empty wasted effort! In fact, we begin to feel a new level of anger over the whole situation.

We are angry at ourselves for investing so much for so long in a relationship with such a poor choice for a spouse.

We are angry at the person to whom we were formerly married, for so miserably failing to keep their vows and completely derailing our dreams for our future life.

Perhaps most of all, we are angry at God for allowing it all to happen. Somehow, we started the journey of life, and the journey of matrimony, under the presumption that if we love our partner enough and love God enough, that it will all work out to fulfill our dreams and expectations. Especially through the hard years of struggling to save a failing relationship, we learned to lean more and more on God, and came to trust Him even when we had learned the marriage partner was untrustworthy. And with that trust came expectations...God was supposed to miraculously heal that marriage relationship and make everything better. He was supposed to bring about the fulfillment of the human dream in our personal life...and He didn't do that! So, we are angry!

At some level all of that anger is a normal healthy part of the grieving process, which helps us to deal with the conflicting emotions and accept the reality of the situation. However, it is important not to continue holding onto the anger past the point of becoming unhealthy, due to choosing to believe a myth rather than believing God's truth.

Biblical Truth:

The error of the myth lies in our human expectations of God, and our assumptions of where His promised faithfulness will lead our lives. The resolution lies in a better understanding of God's promises and of God's heart towards us, His children.

God's Plans are Bigger than Ours:

Let's look, again, at The Great Exodus Story. In the first chapter of Exodus, we read about how "a new king arose over Egypt, who did not know Joseph," (Exodus 1:8) and he enslaved the Israelites, made their lives bitter with hard labor, and ordered their newborn sons to be killed. We read about how, even in this intense persecution, God continued to bless the Israelites and they continued to multiply.

In the second chapter of Exodus, we read the story of Moses' rescue, his adoption as a grandson of Pharaoh, his killing an Egyptian, and his flight to Midian. Then in Exodus 2:23-25, we read of the death of the old Pharaoh, and "the sons of Israel sighed because of the bondage, and they cried out; and their cry for help because of their bondage rose up to God. So God heard their groaning; and God remembered His covenant with Abraham, Isaac, and Jacob. And God saw the sons of Israel and God took notice of them."

The Israelites cried out for help and God heard them. But what did the Israelites have in mind when they cried for help? Was it the same thing God had in mind as He answered? Remember, Israel was in blood covenant with Pharaoh, and had been for almost 430 years. For over 400 years they had lived in Egypt, relied on Pharaoh's provision, and sunk deep roots in the region of Egypt called Goshen.

It is doubtful that very many of this generation of Israelites had a dream or vision of leaving Egypt in a mass exodus and marching across the desert to conquer the Canaanites and occupy the Land of Canaan.

It is much more likely that their vision was to be left in peace by the new Pharaoh, to be allowed to plant their crops, tend their livestock, marry, raise kids, build homes and grow old in peace, right there in Egypt, just as the last ten generations of Israelites had done.

The Israelites cried out for help, hoping God would give the new Pharaoh a tender heart toward them, and grant them peaceful lives in Egypt. God answered, based on God's vision as promised to Abraham more than 500 years earlier, by causing the new Pharaoh's heart to be hardened toward the Israelites, to make their lives more bitter with harder labor. God's plan was not for Israel to have a peaceful life in Egypt, but for God to redeem and deliver them from the bondage of Egypt, and to lead them out to conquer and occupy the land of Canaan!

The difference in perspective shows up time and again throughout the Exodus story. At every obstacle or sign of resistance, the Israelites whine, complain, and say they were better off the way things were before Moses and God showed up. Why? Because they have not, yet, caught God's vision for their destiny. They look back with longing toward

Egypt, because they have not, yet, let go of the vision of living out their lives, peacefully, in Egypt.

God heard their prayers and answered them, far beyond how they imagined! So far beyond their vision, that at first they had trouble recognizing it as an answer to prayer. It looked to them like things were more off-track and more out-of-control than ever before…because they had not yet realized where God was taking them and had not yet adopted God's vision for their lives as their own.

In the same way, we may pour out our hearts to God, for years, asking for His help in a troubled marriage. All the while, we're expecting God to heal a broken relationship…and in many situations, that is exactly how God moves.

However, in other situations, while we are looking for God to heal a relationship, God, instead, is answering our prayers by causing our marriage partner's heart to be hardened against us, for the purpose of bringing about His redemptive work in our lives. When the marriage ends in divorce, we blame God, wondering why He failed to answer our prayers…not recognizing, yet, that He answered our prayers with a vision far greater than ours…a vision of deliverance and redemption!

For a Follower of Christ there is No Such Thing as Wasted Effort or Wasted Love:

In Matthew 25:31-46, Jesus tells about the coming judgment, and separating of the sheep (true believers) from the goats (unbelievers). In verse 40, He says to the sheep, "Truly I say to you, to the extent that you did it to one of these brothers of Mine, even the least of them, you did it to Me."

In 1 John 4:7-8, we are told, "Beloved, let us love one another, for love is from God; and everyone who loves is born of God and knows God. The one who does not love does not know God, for God is love."

In John 15:12-13, Jesus says, "This is My commandment, that you love one another, just as I have loved you. Greater love has no one than this, that one lay down his life for his friends."

God calls us to love people. To love deeply, with abandon. To love sacrificially, laying down our lives for one another.

Jesus promises that, when we love sacrificially, He accepts all that we do as being done for Him!

Think about it! Our greatest and deepest covenant is with God. Our most enduring covenant partner says that all the love we lavish on others, all the work, all the prayers, all the effort, He accepts as being given to Him!

For the believer in Christ, there is no such thing as wasted love or wasted effort. Every gift you gave to the person to whom you were formerly married, Christ accepts as a gift you have given to Him. Every time you chose to set aside your own pride, or your own needs, for the sake of your marriage partner, Jesus accepts as you having made a sacrificial decision for Him. Every tear you shed, Jesus has stored in a bottle (Psalm 56:8). Every prayer you prayed, Jesus accepts as your heart being poured out to Him, in love. And He promises to lavishly pour out His love on you, for all eternity!

All that effort in your previous marriage was not wasted at all. It was a heartfelt offering to your covenant partner, Jesus Christ!

Knowing this, you can choose to love again, unreservedly and unconditionally. Despite all the shattered dreams and broken heart, you can, if you want to, choose to love another marriage partner even more deeply and unreservedly than the first (or to commit yourself to another ministry more zealously than the last).

Why? Because you now know that your deepest covenant partner, Jesus Christ, will be with you through all that you may encounter in life; that He will accept your love offerings as being given to Him; that He will lead you to all the blessing He has stored up for you since before the foundation of the world; and that He will lavish His love on you for all eternity!

Now, go out and meet your destiny in Christ... proudly... fearlessly... with thanksgiving... loving unreservedly... free from the shame of guilt... free from fear of hurt or rejection!

Appendix ~
More about Covenant and Redemption

This appendix is provided as a summary for those who would like to know more about scriptural use of the terms *covenant* and *redemption*. While I consider this to be only a brief summary of a topic that could consume entire books, it provides a significantly more detailed discussion of topics briefly introduced in the Prelude and referenced throughout the text.

Covenant:

A covenant is a formal promise, or promises, made under sacred oath, while solemnly calling on God to witness and enact the covenant. In our modern western society, the ancient tradition of covenant has been largely replaced by legal contracts. However, unlike legal contracts, covenant also includes, and relies on, the relationship formed under the sacred vow as well as God's involvement as judge over the keeping of the covenant.

Ancient Semitic cultures relied on the tradition of covenant as a fundamental fabric of society. For example, if a purchase of land was made, a covenant was cut between the seller and the purchaser, in which the property was deeded over to the seller. However, the covenant did not stop with the transaction. It continued on as a relationship, in which the buyer relied on the seller to defend his ownership rights to the property.

Similarly, a debt or loan was based on a covenant, in which the borrower agreed to repay the loan to the lender. Once the debt was repaid, the debt covenant was ended. However, if the borrower was unable to pay back the loan, then he was required to serve the lender as a slave until such time as the loan could be repaid.

The most sacred of all covenants is the blood covenant, in which two parties are joined as blood brothers, agreeing to defend and protect each other. Through the blood covenant, friends become mutual friends, family becomes mutual family, and enemies become mutual enemies. In the case of marriage, which is considered a blood covenant, "the two shall become one flesh" (Matthew 19:5).

Kingdoms are based on a blood covenant between the king and the people of the kingdom, such as the covenant described in 2 Samuel 5:3 as being cut between King David and the Kingdom of Israel.

Covenants are an inheritance, passed down from father to son. It is through this covenant inheritance that ownership of property is passed to the next generation. Likewise a debt covenant is passed from father to son, and the son is responsible for repaying his father's debts. In the same way, it is through covenant inheritance that an heir to the throne is established upon the death of a king.

Many traditions, rich in symbolism, surround the ancient rite of cutting a covenant. A blood covenant often included a letting and mixing of blood, rubbing dirt or ink into the wound to form a permanent scar or tattoo, *the mark of the covenant*.

The covenant ceremony frequently included a covenant meal. The covenant meal included drinking red wine to represent partaking of each other's life, and eating bread to symbolizing partaking of each other's nature.

A blood covenant ceremony often included an exchange of clothes and of weapons, indicating a putting on of each other's nature, strength, and protection. It also often included an exchange of names, in which a covenant partner was given a new name, indicating that their identity had been changed in association with their new covenant partner.

A blood covenant ceremony sometimes included a *walk through death* in which animals were killed and cut in half with the halves laid out on either side of an aisle down the middle. The covenant partners would then walk a figure-eight through the halves of the animal carcasses, while reciting solemn vows, calling on God as witness, pointing at the dead animals, declaring, "Thus may the Lord do to me, and worse, if anything but death parts you and me" (Ruth 1:17).

The *walk through death* represented a dying to their former life and beginning a new life as one with their covenant partner. From this moment on, they counted themselves dead to their former life and alive to a new life with their covenant partner.

In the New Testament Church, believer baptism carries symbolism very similar to the *walk through death*. The Apostle Paul said, in regard to the covenant rite of baptism, "...consider yourselves to be dead to sin, but alive to God in Christ Jesus" (Romans 6:11).

Not all of these traditions were included in every covenant ceremony, and not all rites included in a given ceremony were necessarily recorded in the biblical text. Covenant relationships are denoted in scripture, not only by direct use of the word *covenant*, but also by reference to covenant terminology or specific traditions typical of a covenant ceremony.

As one example of this, in the account of Saul's conversion after being struck blind on the road to Damascus, Ananias, a disciple living in Damascus, was sent to speak to Saul (later called Paul). "So Ananias departed and entered the house, and after laying his hands on him said, 'Brother Saul, the Lord Jesus, who appeared to you on the road by which you were coming, has sent me so that you may regain your sight and be filled with the Holy Spirit.' And immediately there fell from his eyes something like scales, and he regained his sight, and he got up and was baptized; and he took food and was strengthened" (Acts 9:17-19).

Note that this passage makes no specific mention of Saul repenting of his sins, confessing Jesus as Christ, or entering a covenant with God through faith in Christ. We are simply told that he was baptized. We understand that this was believer's baptism and that it was administered pursuant to Saul's acceptance of Jesus as Lord of his life. However, the covenant with God which Saul entered into, by faith in Christ, is implied by reference to the covenant rite of baptism, rather than by explicit statement. Since we are familiar with the covenant rite of baptism, the implication is clear to us, and we would not even think to question what it meant. However, if we were unfamiliar with the practice of believer baptism, then the implication would be less obvious.

This sort of reference to a covenant by mention of covenant traditions or covenant terminology is very common in scripture. Such references are not always as clear to us, to whom the traditions are unfamiliar, as they were to people of the time and culture in which they were written.

Not only is covenant referenced by mention of common covenant rites or traditions, but also by use of covenant terminology, that is use of words which are commonly used in reference to a covenant relationship. In studying covenant, in scripture, it is helpful to keep in mind some of the common words used in reference to covenant:

1. *Friend*: Jesus said to the disciples, "No longer do I call you slaves, for the slave does not know what his master is doing; but I have called you *friends*, for all things that I have heard from My Father I have made known to you" (John 15:15).

2. *Beloved*: "Like an apple tree among the trees of the forest, so is my *beloved* among the young men. In his shade I took great delight and sat down, and his fruit was sweet to my taste. He has brought me to his banquet hall, and his banner over me is love" (Song of Solomon 2:3-4).

3. *Lovingkindness*: "The Lord has made known His salvation; He has revealed righteousness in the sight of the nations. He has remembered His *lovingkindness* and His faithfulness to the house of Israel" (Psalm 98:2-3).

4. *Child* (son, adoption): "But as many as received Him, to them He gave the right to become *children* of God..." (John 1:12). "Because you are *sons*, God has sent forth the Spirit of His Son into our hearts, crying, 'Abba! Father!' Therefore you are no longer a slave, but a *son*; and if a *son*, then an heir through God" (Galatians 4:6-7).

5. *Father* (Abba): "For you have not received a spirit of slavery to fear again, but have received a spirit of adoption as sons by which we cry out, "*Abba*! *Father*!" (Romans 8:15).

6. *Know* (knew, known of): "If you had *known* Me, you would have *known* My Father also; from now on you *know* Him, and have seen Him." (John 14:7). "But now that you have come to *know* God, or rather to be *known by* God, how is it that you turn back again to the weak and worthless elemental things, to which you desire to be enslaved all over again?" (Galatians 4:9). "Now Adam *knew* Eve his wife, and she conceived and bore Cain..." (Genesis 4:1, *NKJV*). "Many will say to Me on that day, 'Lord, Lord, did we not prophesy in Your name, and in Your name cast out demons, and in Your name perform many miracles?' And then I will declare to them, 'I never *knew* you; depart from Me, you who practice lawlessness'"(Matthew 7:22-23).

7. *Circumcised* (Circumcision, Mark of the Covenant): "Now as for you, you shall keep My covenant, you and your descendants after you throughout their generations. This is My covenant, which you shall keep, between Me and you and your descendants after you: every male among you shall be *circumcised*. And you shall be *circumcised* in the flesh of your foreskin, and it shall be the *sign of the covenant* between Me and you" (Genesis 17:7-11). "...and in Him you were also *circumcised* with a *circumcision* made without hands, in the removal of the body of the flesh by the *circumcision* of Christ; having been buried with Him in baptism, in which you were also raised up with Him through faith

in the working of God, who raised Him from the dead" (Colossians 2:11-12).

8. *Remember* (Faithfulness, not Forget): "The Lord has made known His salvation; He has revealed righteousness in the sight of the nations. He has *remembered* His lovingkindness and His *faithfulness* to the house of Israel" (Psalm 98:2-3). "Can a woman forget her nursing child and have no compassion on the son of her womb? Even these may forget, but I will *not forget* you. Behold, I have inscribed you on the palms of My hands" (Isaiah 49:15-16).

The Bible is full of examples of covenant and of covenant references. Some of the more significant biblical covenants include the following:

1. Adam was created in covenant with God (Genesis 1:27 & 2:7, Hosea 6:7).

2. When Adam sinned, he entered into covenant with the kingdom of darkness (Isaiah 28:15-18). Pursuant to Adam's sin, scripture frequently refers to the relationship of mankind (Adam's heirs) with the kingdom of darkness (a.k.a. sin, death, Sheol, deception, lies, the world, the flesh, father of lies, the evil one, or prince of darkness) in terms of a blood covenant relationship.

3. After the great flood, God made a covenant with the earth, setting the rainbow as the mark of the covenant (Genesis 9:8-17).

4. God cut a covenant with Abraham, in which God, himself, walked the figure-eight *walk through death*, and gave Abraham a new name and the sign of

circumcision as the mark of the covenant (Genesis 15:1-21 & 17:1-22).

5. Pharaoh cut a covenant with Joseph, through which Joseph's father, Jacob (Israel), and his family were later granted property in Egypt and provision during the seven-year famine (Genesis 41:39-45).

6. God cut a covenant with the Nation of Israel through which He became their God and Israel became His people (Exodus 24:1-11). The terms of the covenant (the ten commandments) were carved in stone tablets and placed inside the sacred Ark of the Covenant.

7. Jesus cut a new covenant with the Father, on our behalf, through the shedding of His own blood and the tearing of His own flesh (Matthew 26:26-28 & Hebrews 9:1-28).

Redemption:

The most common definition provided for the word *redemption* is *to buy back*. However, in studying the use of this word in scripture, this simplified definition is found lacking. While it does provide a nice simple definition for many instances of scriptural redemption, it does not adequately define the word as used in the most significant biblical redemptions. A more accurate definition of *redemption*, as used in scripture, would be *to justly bring about the end of a covenant of bondage by which someone or something belonging to God is being held captive.*

Keeping in mind that the purchase and ownership of property was covenant based, and that debt was covenant based, for most common life circumstances involving redemption, the simplified definition and the more accurate definition could be applicably used interchangeably.

However, as will become apparent as we further explore this topic, the simplified definition, *to buy back*, does not fit the case of redemption from a blood covenant which has become bondage.

God provided redemption right for land that had been sold (Leviticus 25:23-34) so that the land could be bought back by the original land owner, or by a near kinsman on his behalf. Essentially, the redemption right allowed the seller to cancel the purchase covenant by refunding the cost of the sale.

In the agrarian society of Old Testament Israel, the ownership of land was essential to livelihood, and the loss of land ownership could leave a family destitute. However, the basis of the requirement of provision for redemption was that the land belongs to God, "The land, moreover, shall not be sold permanently, for the land is Mine; for you are but aliens and sojourners with Me. Thus for every piece of your property, you are to provide for the redemption of the land" (Leviticus 25:23-24).

God also provided redemption right for someone who had become enslaved as the result of a debt covenant that he could not repay (Leviticus 25:47-55). A near kinsman could redeem the debtor from slavery by repaying the debt on his behalf. The debt payment justly fulfilled the covenant obligation, thus ending the debt covenant. Here, again, the basis given for the redemption right was that they belong to God, "For they are My servants whom I brought out from the land of Egypt…" (Leviticus 25:42).

The Story of the Great Exodus

~ *Redemption of a Nation* ~

Pharaoh cut a covenant with Joseph in a ceremony described in Genesis 41:39-45. All subjects of a king are in blood covenant with the king, but the ceremony described and the resulting relationship between Joseph and Pharaoh clearly go far beyond that of a normal subject of the crown, to a blood covenant in which Joseph was treated as an equal to Pharaoh.

Joseph was given a new name, new clothes, a gold necklace, new authority, and Pharaoh's own signet ring. As discussed above, the new clothes and new name carried significant meaning in a blood covenant ceremony, and the signet ring, in particular, gave Joseph full authority to speak on behalf of Pharaoh. A command issued by Joseph, under the seal of Pharaoh's signet ring carried the full authority of Pharaoh's own signature. Pharaoh said that Joseph was now ruler over all the land of Egypt, and equal to Pharaoh in everything except the throne. Though the word *covenant* is not explicitly used in this passage, it is clear both by reference to covenant rites and by transfer of trust and authority, that Joseph entered into blood covenant with Pharaoh, King of Egypt.

Later, Joseph's father, brothers, and family moved to Egypt, in order to escape starvation during the seven years of famine. By accepting Pharaoh's provision, they accepted the protection of Pharaoh's covenant with Joseph, placing themselves under obligation to that covenant.

Moreover, since covenant is an inheritance from father to son, all of Israel's descendants and all of Pharaoh's descendants were in blood covenant with each other. They were *family*, blood-brothers.

The book of Exodus begins, in Exodus 1:8, with these words, "Now a new king arose over Egypt, who did not *know* Joseph."

The Hebrew word translated here as *know (yada`)* is used almost exclusively to denote either the intimate personal empathetic understanding of a covenant partner or special God-given perceptive understanding of a specific topic. This is the same word used, for example, in Genesis 4:1 (*NKJV*), "Now Adam *knew* Eve his wife, and she conceived and bore Cain..." In this case, it is clearly a covenant reference, indicating that the new Pharaoh was not empathetically disposed toward the family of his covenant partner, Joseph.

The new Pharaoh chose not to honor the covenant with Joseph (did not *know* Joseph). Rather than acting on behalf of his covenant partners, as was his obligation by sacred oath, he chose rather to enslave them. Because of the change of attitude on the part of the new Pharaoh, Israel was now in a covenant that had become bondage, or slavery. They were in need of redemption from their covenant with Pharaoh, and they had no means of redeeming themselves.

God told Moses, "Say, therefore, to the sons of Israel, 'I am the Lord, and I will bring you out from under the burdens of the Egyptians, and I will *deliver* you from their bondage. I will also *redeem* you with an outstretched arm and with great judgments'" (Exodus 6:6).

Note that God listed *deliver* and *redeem* as two separate actions He would perform on behalf of His people, Israel. To this day, Jewish Passover traditions, designed by God to commemorate this historic event, include four cups of wine to be drunk at specific intervals in the meal, with the cup of *redemption* and the cup of *deliverance* recognized as two separate acts to be celebrated. Nor is this unique to the Exodus story. The words *deliver* and *redeem* are often paired in scripture as two separate but closely related actions or events (Job 6:23, Jeremiah 15:21).

Deliverance speaks of God's protection and provision as Israel was brought out of Egypt and journeyed to the promised land. *Redemption* speaks of Israel being justly released from their covenant obligations to Pharaoh.

God's plan for Israel, as revealed to Moses, was to redeem Israel from their blood covenant with Pharaoh. When Israel left Egypt, they were to leave with no covenant ties, no covenant obligations, no debts or allegiance owed to Pharaoh.

But what was the redemption payment? At what price was the covenant obligation fulfilled? How can a price even be set for a blood covenant? Did God pay Pharaoh some ransom price for the freedom of Israel?

God said He would redeem Israel, "with an outstretched arm and with great judgments."

In reading the Exodus story, three truths stand out clearly:

1. God was in complete control from start to finish. Even when Pharaoh appears to be in the position of authority, God is working out His plan through Pharaoh's choices.

2. Israel was not leaving Egypt without Pharaoh's permission, not even for a few days. Over and over, God sent Moses back to Pharaoh asking permission for Israel to leave Egypt for just a few days.

3. Israel was not leaving Egypt with Pharaoh's blessing. Each time, God caused Pharaoh's heart to be

hardened, so that Pharaoh refused to let Israel go, even as plague after plague continued to roll over the land of Egypt.

God could have delivered Israel without Pharaoh's permission. So, why was Pharaoh's permission required? And why, if Pharaoh's permission was required, did God cause Pharaoh's heart to be hardened, so that he consistently refused to let Israel go, until after the plague of the death of the first-born?

The answers are found in Exodus 6:1, "Then the Lord said to Moses, 'Now you shall see what I will do to Pharaoh; for under compulsion he will let them go, and under compulsion he will drive them out of his land.'"

When Pharaoh chose to "drive them out of his land" Israel was released from their covenant obligation. At that moment, Israel was divorced from Egypt. The covenant was dissolved, and Israel was free to proceed to the Promised Land with no obligation of allegiance to Egypt.

In fact, the Hebrew words translated here as the phrases *let them go* (*shalach*) and *drive them out* (*garash*) are both translated elsewhere as *divorce* (Malachi 2:16, Leviticus 21:14).

By the manner in which God redeemed Israel from Egypt, He gave new meaning to the word *redemption*. No ransom price was paid, yet the covenant of bondage was dissolved, in a manner that was just. As their redeemer, God justly caused Israel's blood covenant with Egypt to be dissolved, so that Israel was no longer in a covenant of bondage to Egypt.

God brought about the divorce of Israel from Egypt, and God called it *redemption*.

The Story of the Second Great Exodus

~ Redemption of Mankind ~

The New Testament tells another story of redemption, the redemption of the race of mankind from Adam's covenant with the kingdom of darkness.

The Bible tells us much about the earthly ministry of Jesus and the work that Christ accomplished on the cross. It tells us very little of what happened during the three days that Jesus was in the grave.

The story recorded in Exodus, of Israel's redemption from their covenant with Egypt, is both a record of an historical event and a picture foretelling how Christ would redeem mankind from Adam's covenant with the kingdom of darkness. We have been given the details of how God dealt with Egypt, *with an outstretched arm and with great judgments.* We can surmise that the judgments of Christ, *the Arm of the Lord* (Isaiah 53:1) in Sheol (the place of the dead) were as compelling to Satan as the centuries earlier judgments of plagues had been to Pharaoh.

This much we know for certain: Jesus redeemed us from Adam's covenant of bondage to the kingdom of darkness, and in that redemption no ransom payment was made to Satan.

Lest anyone misunderstand, let me hasten to clarify that Jesus paid a tremendous price for our salvation. He left the glory of Heaven to become flesh and dwell among men. He suffered physical torture and death. He bore our sins on the cross, suffering the consequences of sin on our behalf. He made atonement for our transgressions. Through the pouring out of His own life blood and the rending of His own flesh, Jesus cut a new covenant with the Father on our behalf.

I do not want to minimize, in any way, the tremendous sacrifice that Jesus made for us and through which He justly brought about the end of our covenant of bondage to the kingdom of darkness, while enacting a new covenant with the Father, through which we might be restored to right relationship with God.

However, no ransom payment was made to the kingdom of darkness from which we were redeemed. Justice was done and that justice was tremendously costly. Yet, when Jesus led the exodus from Sheol, the only thing delivered to Satan was a *Paid in Full* notice.

Just as God brought about the divorce of Israel from Egypt, Jesus brought about mankind's divorce from the kingdom of darkness, and called it *redemption*.

What does Jesus look like going through a divorce?

He looks much as He did leading the exodus of His people out through the gates of Sheol! Acting as our kinsman-redeemer, justly redeeming His children from covenants of bondage, Jesus walks with us as He delivers us through the divorce.

Thank God, He is still in the business of redeeming His children from covenants of bondage!

ABOUT THE AUTHOR

A student of the Bible since early childhood, Joseph Pote (Joe) was literally raised in church, attending multiple church services and Bible studies each week. Having also endured the devastation of a failed marriage, Joe combines a sound understanding of biblical principles with personal experience of the issues and concerns of believers who have experienced divorce.

An Arkansas native, Joe currently lives on a small family farm outside Hope, Arkansas, with his wife Sherri, and two stepsons. In addition to stepsons, Tyler and Dawson, Joe has four grown children, Tabitha, Timothy, Amelia and Naomi, as well as five grandchildren, Thaddeus, Tristen, Ethan, Hannah, and Katelyn.

In addition to enjoying the creativity of his profession as a structural engineer, in his leisure time Joe enjoys reading, hiking, camping and gardening, especially with children and grandchildren. He is active in church children's ministries as well as in Sunday school. He would like for you to visit his website at www.josephjpote.com

94357391R00052

Made in the USA
Lexington, KY
27 July 2018